|| THE WORLD OF MUSIC ||

Jazz Music

Published by Creative Education
P.O. Box 227
Mankato, Minnesota 56002
Creative Education is an imprint of The Creative Company.

DESIGN AND PRODUCTION BY **ZENO DESIGN**

PHOTOGRAPHS BY Corbis (Bettmann; Dat's Jazz; Lynn Goldsmith; Robert
Holmes; Hulton-Deutsch Collection; Kelly-Mooney; Derick A. Thomas),
Getty Images (Brad Barket; Tom Copi/Michael Ochs Archives; Bert Hardy/
Picture Post; Medioimages/Photodisc)

LIBRARY OF CONGRESS CATALOGING-IN-PUBLICATION DATA

Riggs, Kate.
Jazz music / by Kate Riggs.
p. cm. — (World of music)
Includes index.
ISBN 978-1-58341-567-2
1. Jazz—History and criticism—Juvenile literature. I. Title.

ML3506.R54 2008
781.65—dc22   2006102984

First edition

9 8 7 6 5 4 3 2 1

Jazz

MUSIC

KATE RIGGS

CREATIVE EDUCATION

Jazz music is a cool kind of music. It started almost 100 years ago. It uses rhythms (*RIH-thumz*) that are fast and bouncy. People from Africa brought the rhythms to the United States. They sang the songs while they worked.

Many Africans first came to the United States as slaves.

People can play jazz music on guitars

People sing jazz music. They play it on instruments, too. The trumpet is a jazz instrument. It is made out of metal. It can make high, tooting sounds. Sometimes it is very loud!

Trumpets are shiny instruments

A man named Louis (*LOO-ee*) Armstrong played trumpet. He sang, too. He was one of the first great jazz musicians (*mew-ZIH-shuns*). He loved to sing and play for people.

Louis Armstrong sang a famous song called "What a Wonderful World."

Louis Armstrong smiled big when he sang

Many people who played jazz music played at places called jazz clubs. Every band wanted to play at a club. That was where they could play in front of lots of people. They would go to big cities just to play at a club.

Lots of people play jazz in a city called New Orleans (NEW OR-linz).

Jazz clubs have colorful signs

Soon, people started dancing to jazz music. Jazz bands got bigger. They used more instruments. The saxophone was a loud jazz instrument. It could blast out lots of sounds!

Some saxophones are small, like this one

Jazz music has rules. Rules tell people how to play something. But people who play jazz like to bend the rules. They like to make up music as they are playing. That is what makes jazz different from other kinds of music.

A man named Duke Ellington wrote hundreds of jazz songs.

Jazz trumpets come in different shapes

Some jazz music is jumpy. Some jazz is very smooth. Some is fast and happy. Other jazz music is slow and sad. Every jazz song is different.

Swing music is a kind of jazz. People like to dance to swing.

Charlie Parker played jumpy jazz music

A woman named Ella Fitzgerald sang lots of jazz songs. People liked her deep, smooth voice. She could sing high notes. She could sing low notes. People called her the "First Lady of Song."

Jazz singer Ella Fitzgerald

Lots of people like jazz music. They play it in jazz bands. They sing along with the songs. Some people just sit and listen to it. There are lots of ways to enjoy the cool sounds of jazz.

People like to clap their hands when they listen to jazz. It is okay to make noise!

Jazz bands have lots of instruments

GLOSSARY

Africa a big, hot land that is across the ocean

instruments things people play to make music

rhythms patterns of beats found in music

saxophone an instrument made out of metal; it is shaped like the letter "J"

slaves people who were owned by other people; they were not free to do what they wanted to do

Some jazz musicians play big bass guitars

INDEX

Africa 4

Armstrong, Louis 8

Ellington, Duke 14

Fitzgerald, Ella 18

jazz bands 10, 12, 20

jazz clubs 10

New Orleans 10

rules 14

saxophones 12

slaves 4

swing music 16

trumpets 6, 8

United States 4